I Love My Pet
FERRET

Aaron Carr

LET'S READ
AV2 BY WEIGL™
ADDED VALUE · AUDIO VISUAL

Go to **www.av2books.com**, and enter this book's unique code.

BOOK CODE

R516756

AV² by Weigl brings you media enhanced books that support active learning.

AV² provides enriched content that supplements and complements this book. Weigl's AV² books strive to create inspired learning and engage young minds in a total learning experience.

Your AV² Media Enhanced books come alive with...

Audio
Listen to sections of the book read aloud.

Key Words
Study vocabulary, and complete a matching word activity.

Video
Watch informative video clips.

Quizzes
Test your knowledge.

Embedded Weblinks
Gain additional information for research.

Slide Show
View images and captions, and prepare a presentation.

Try This!
Complete activities and hands-on experiments.

...and much, much more!

Published by AV² by Weigl
350 5th Avenue, 59th Floor New York, NY 10118
Website: www.av2books.com www.weigl.com

Library of Congress Cataloguing in Publication data available upon request.
Fax 1-866-449-3445 for the attention of the Publishing Records department.

ISBN 978-1-62127-292-2 (hardcover)
ISBN 978-1-62127-298-4 (softcover)

Printed in the United States of America in North Mankato, Minnesota
1 2 3 4 5 6 7 8 9 0 16 15 14 13 12

122012
WEP301112

Senior Editor: Aaron Carr   Art Director: Terry Paulhus

Weigl acknowledges Getty Images as the primary image supplier for this title.

W 23.99 may 2/14

2

I Love My Pet
FERRET

CONTENTS

I love my pet ferret.
I take good care of her.

My pet ferret could fit in
a teaspoon when she was born.
She could not open her eyes
for about a month.

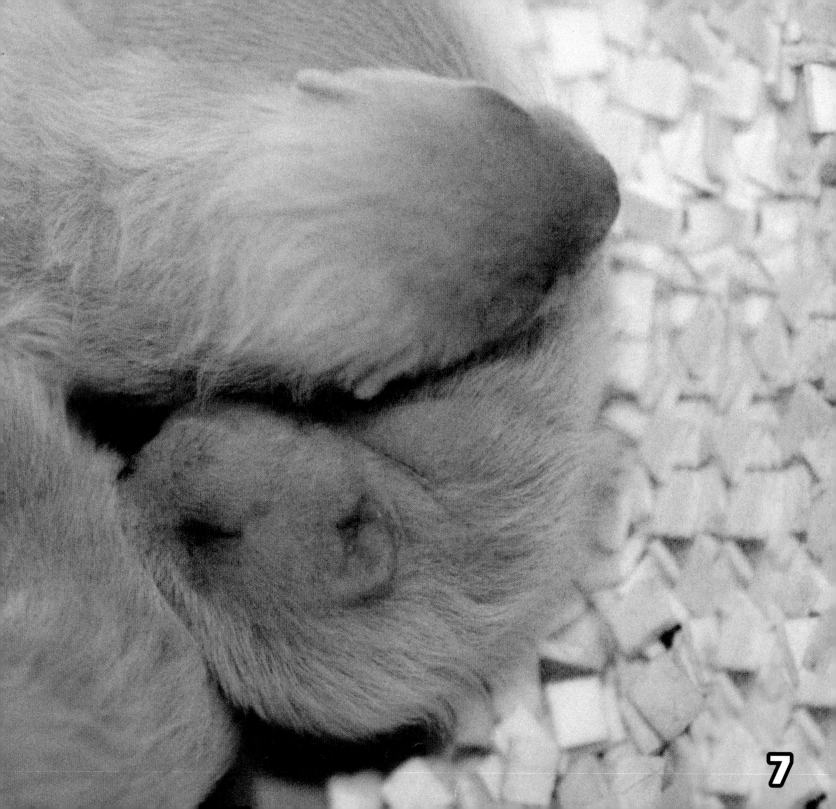

My pet ferret was eight weeks old
when I brought her home.
She was full grown after six months.

Ferrets can grow up to 2 feet long.

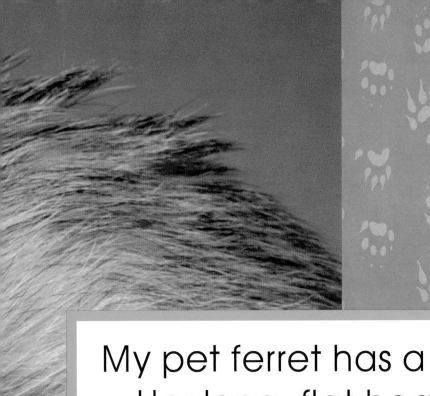

My pet ferret has a long, flat head. Her long, flat head helps her fit into small spaces.

My pet ferret
has long, sharp teeth.
Her sharp teeth
help her eat meat.

A ferret's teeth
may turn yellow
as it gets older.

My pet ferret needs to eat every few hours. I make sure her food bowl is never empty.

Eating chocolate, nuts, garlic, and onions can make a ferret sick.

16

My pet ferret is very playful.
She likes to run, dig,
and play with her toys.

My pet ferret
needs help staying clean.
It is my job to keep
her cage clean.

I make sure
my pet ferret is healthy.
I love my pet ferret.

21

FERRET FACTS

These pages provide more detail about the interesting facts found in the book. They are intended to be used by adults as a learning support to help young readers round out their knowledge of each animal featured in the *I Love My Pet* series.

Pages 4–5

I love my pet ferret. I take good care of her. Ferrets may look like rodents, but they are actually related to the weasel family. Ferrets make excellent pets. They are the third most popular pet in the United States, with about 10 million pet ferrets in homes across the country. Ferrets are smart animals and can even learn tricks.

Pages 6–7

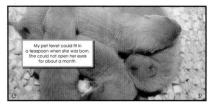

My pet ferret could fit in a teaspoon when she was born. She could not open her eyes for about a month. Ferret mothers give birth to five or six babies, or kits, at one time. Kits are about 2 inches (5 centimeters) long at birth. They are born with their eyes closed, and their fur is very thin, causing the kit's pink skin to show through.

Pages 8–9

My pet ferret was eight weeks old when I brought her home. She was full grown after six months. About three to four weeks after birth, kits open their eyes, and their fur grows into a full coat. By eight weeks of age, ferrets are ready to go to a new home. Full-grown ferrets can weigh 1 to 3 pounds (0.5 to 1.4 kilograms) for females, or jills, and 3 to 5 pounds (1.4 to 2.3 kg) for males, or hobs.

Pages 10–11

My pet ferret has a long, flat head. Her long, flat head helps her fit into small spaces. Ferrets also have short, strong legs that help them move in tight spaces. Ferrets can squeeze through holes just 1 inch (2.5 cm) wide. In Ancient Rome, hunters sent ferrets into underground tunnels and burrows to chase rabbits into the open. This was called ferreting.

Pages 12–13

My pet ferret has long, sharp teeth. Her sharp teeth help her eat meat. Ferrets have four kinds of teeth. They have four long, sharp teeth, called canines, that are used for tearing meat. On each side of the mouth, 12 premolars and six molars are used to chew food. Ferrets also have 12 small teeth, called incisors, between their canines that are used for grooming.

Pages 14–15

My pet ferret needs to eat every few hours. I make sure her food bowl is never empty. Ferrets are carnivores, or meat-eaters. They need to eat every three to four hours, so it is important to make sure their food dish is never empty. Ferrets also need a steady supply of fresh, clean water. For a treat, ferrets can have cooked chicken or beef, as long as the bones have been removed.

Pages 16–17

My pet ferret is very playful. She likes to run, dig, and play with her toys. Ferrets spend 18 to 20 hours sleeping each day. While awake, however, they are very active. Ferrets need plenty of exercise to stay healthy. They like to run and dig. Ferrets also like to play chasing or tugging games with their owners or other ferrets. Ferrets should be given a few hours each day to run around.

Pages 18–19

My pet ferret needs help staying clean. It is my job to keep her cage clean. Ferrets will usually keep themselves clean. If they do get dirty, they may need a bath. Avoid bathing ferrets too often, as this can cause the ferret to lose natural oils from its skin. This can cause a strong, musky odor. Ferrets will need their nails clipped every one to two weeks.

Pages 20–21

I make sure my pet ferret is healthy. I love my pet ferret. With proper care, ferrets can live between six and eight years. Ferrets need to be checked by a veterinarian every year, and they may need vaccines to keep them from getting sick. Like dogs, ferrets can get fleas. However, dog flea treatments can harm ferrets. If you are unsure what to do for your ferret, always ask a veterinarian.

KEY WORDS

Research has shown that as much as 65 percent of all written material published in English is made up of 300 words. These 300 words cannot be taught using pictures or learned by sounding them out. They must be recognized by sight. This book contains 51 common sight words to help young readers improve their reading fluency and comprehension. This book also teaches young readers several important content words, such as proper nouns. These words are paired with pictures to aid in learning and improve understanding.

Page	Sight Words First Appearance
4	good, her, I, my, of, take
6	a, about, could, eyes, for, in, not, open, she, was, when
9	after, can, feet, grown, home, long, old, to, up
11	has, head, helps, into, small
12	as, eat, gets, it, may, turn
15	and, every, few, food, is, make, needs, never
17	likes, run, very, with
18	keep

Page	Content Words First Appearance
4	care, ferret, pet
6	month, teaspoon
9	eight, six, weeks
11	spaces
12	meat, sharp, teeth, yellow
15	bowl, chocolate, garlic, hours, nuts, onions, sick
17	toys
18	cage, clean, job
21	healthy

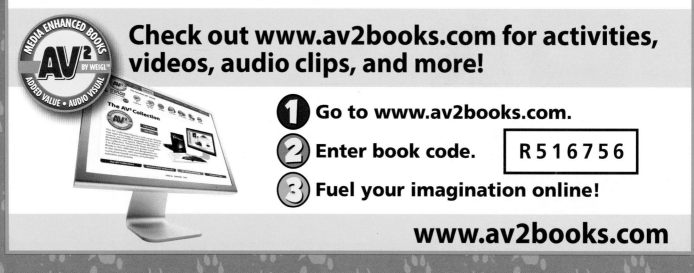